Compulsive Overeating

Perspectives on Mental Health

by Judith Peacock

Consultant:
Barbara DeJonge, MA, LP, LICSW
Fairview University Medical Center
Adolescent Eating Disorder Program
Minneapolis, Minnesota

LifeMatters
an imprint of Capstone Press
Mankato, Minnesota

LifeMatters Books are published by Capstone Press
PO Box 669 • 151 Good Counsel Drive • Mankato, Minnesota 56002
http://www.capstone-press.com

Printed in the United States of America

Library of Congress Cataloging-in-Publication Data
Peacock, Judith, 1942-
      Compulsive overeating / by Judith Peacock.
          p. cm. — (Perspectives on mental health)
      Includes bibliographical references and index.
      Summary: Examines the phenomenon of compulsive overeating, various causes, and strategies for dealing with this disorder in oneself and others.
      ISBN 0-7368-0437-4 (book) — ISBN 0-7368-0440-4 (series)
      1. Compulsive eating —Juvenile literature. 2. Compulsive eaters—Juvenile literature. 3. Eating disorders—Juvenile literature. [1. Compulsive eating. 2. Eating disorders.] I. Title. II. Series.
      RC552.C65 P43 2000   99-054355
      616.85′26—dc21   CIP

Staff Credits
Marta Fahrenz, editor; Adam Lazar, designer; Jodi Theisen, photo researcher

Photo Credits
Cover: ©Capstone Press/Adam Lazar
FPG International/©Dennie Cody, 48; ©James Levin, 56; ©Bill Losh, 19; ©Barbara Peacock, 9
Index Stock/24; 31; 46; 55
International Stock/©Scott Barrow, 37; ©Patrick Ramsey, 7
Photo Network/©Esbin-Anderson, 22
Photri/©Skjold, 14
Uniphoto Picture Agency/©Llewellyn, 17, 52
Visuals Unlimited/©Jeff Greenberg, 38

A 0 9 8 7 6 5 4 3 2 1

Table of Contents

Compulsive overeating is a type of eating disorder. People who compulsively overeat consume a large amount of food in a short period. This is called binge eating.

People who compulsively overeat lack control during a binge. They eat more rapidly than normal, and they usually eat alone. They eat even though they may not be physically hungry.

During a binge, people who compulsively overeat feel calm and comforted. Afterward, they may feel guilty or ashamed. People who compulsively overeat do not purge, or rid their body of food, after eating.

Bulimia nervosa and anorexia nervosa are two other types of eating disorders. People with bulimia binge and then purge. People with anorexia starve themselves.

Low self-esteem and fear of being fat are common to all eating disorders.

Chapter 1

What Is Compulsive Overeating?

Friday night at last! Trish has the apartment to herself. She surveys her feast: fried chicken, potato salad, shrimp salad, and rice pudding. Plus a dozen sugar doughnuts and a gallon of chocolate ice cream.

TRISH, AGE 16

Trish fills a plate with food and sits in front of the TV. The Friday night movie blares as she chews and swallows. All the loneliness and hurt of the past week melt away as the food slides down Trish's throat. She feels warm and protected.

Later, only one chicken breast remains. Trish throws the garbage in the dumpster. She doesn't want her parents to know what she's been doing. Her mother already thinks Trish is too fat.

People who compulsively overeat are likely to be compulsive about other things as well. For example, they may shop compulsively. They have an uncontrollable urge to buy things they don't need or want or can't afford.

Trish has an eating disorder called compulsive overeating. Another name for compulsive overeating is binge-eating disorder. A compulsion is a strong urge to do something. People who compulsively overeat cannot stop themselves from eating. They consume more food than their body wants or needs. However, their overeating is a symptom, or sign, of other problems. Often these problems are emotional in nature.

Characteristics of Compulsive Overeating

Everyone overeats from time to time. Overeating is common on special occasions or during get-togethers with friends. Who can resist an extra helping of turkey or an extra piece of pumpkin pie at Thanksgiving? A favorite food also might tempt a person to overeat. You might love chocolate chip cookies. You tell yourself that you are going to eat only one. Then you end up eating six or seven.

While occasional overeating is normal, compulsive overeating is not. People who compulsively overeat have an unhealthy relationship with food. They show some or all of the characteristics described in the next paragraphs.

Repeated Episodes of Binge Eating

People who compulsively overeat may limit themselves to normal or small amounts of food for a while. Then they go on a binge. During a binge, they eat huge amounts of food in a short period of time. For example, they might consume 3,000 calories in 30 minutes. (Adults normally consume an average of 2,000 to 2,500 calories per day.) People who compulsively overeat may binge several times a week. During a binge, people who compulsively overeat generally crave foods high in salt, sugar, and fat. Examples include pie, cake, cookies, doughnuts, and potato chips. Some people who compulsively overeat binge on a specific food, such as ice cream. Some may binge only on a certain brand of ice cream.

Some people who compulsively overeat do not consume a huge amount in one sitting. Instead, they may eat small amounts all day long. They nibble constantly.

Eating Rapidly

During an episode of binge eating, people eat more rapidly than normal. In their hurry, they may stuff food into their mouth with their hands. They may not even taste the food in their haste to eat.

People who compulsively overeat may seem to be starving. However, they usually are not physically hungry. Instead, they are desperate to fill an emotional emptiness.

Some experts say that binge-eating disorder affects from 2 to 5 percent of the United States population. Bulimia affects from 1 to 3 percent, and anorexia less than 1 percent.

Bingeing Alone

People who compulsively overeat generally binge alone. They may feel ashamed and embarrassed by how much they eat or how they behave. They do not want other people to see them.

People who compulsively overeat often try to keep their bingeing a secret. They hide food around the house or sneak food from the refrigerator. They even may lie or make excuses about their eating behavior.

BRIANA, AGE 15

Briana leads a desperate double life. During the day, when she's with family and friends, she eats a normal amount of food. At night, when she's alone, she compulsively overeats.

Briana hides snack cakes and candy bars in her backpack. She has a stash of cookies, pretzels, and potato chips under her bed. Briana locks herself in her bedroom. Her parents think she's studying. However, Briana is listening to music and eating.

At night when everybody is in bed, Briana raids the refrigerator. She takes a little of each leftover so that her mother won't know anything is missing.

Lack of Control During a Binge

Once people who compulsively overeat start bingeing, they often cannot stop. They eat too much even though they realize it may be harmful. They keep eating even though their stomach hurts. People who compulsively overeat for several years may get used to the physical discomfort. They may lose the ability to tell when their stomach is full.

Self-Hatred and Disgust After a Binge

People who compulsively overeat usually feel calm and comforted while bingeing. Like alcohol or other drugs, the food may give them a high. After the binge, however, they crash. They may hate themselves for overeating and vow never to do it again. They usually feel tired and dull from all the food they have eaten.

No Purging

People who compulsively overeat do not purge, or rid the body of food, after bingeing. Purging is usually done by vomiting or using laxatives. A laxative is a drug that loosens the body's waste so that it can be eliminated quickly. Most people who compulsively overeat do not work off the extra calories by exercising. Weight gain is a natural consequence of compulsive overeating.

Compulsive Overeating and Other Eating Disorders

Compulsive overeating, or binge-eating disorder, is one of three major eating disorders. The other two are bulimia nervosa and anorexia nervosa. People with bulimia also binge, but then purge. People with anorexia eat little or no food. They starve themselves.

Some experts believe that binge-eating disorder is three times more common than anorexia and twice as common as bulimia. Like bulimia and anorexia, compulsive overeating affects more females than males. However, males make up 30 to 35 percent of those who compulsively overeat. Experts believe that eating disorders in boys are often overlooked or ignored. Boys may feel more pressure than girls to handle problems and not to talk about their emotions. Boys may stuff feelings of sadness or depression through compulsive overeating.

Common Characteristics

People who have eating disorders share some characteristics. Many dislike their body and have low self-esteem. This means they don't like or value themselves. They fear being fat. People with anorexia deny themselves food to keep from gaining weight. People with bulimia purge to keep from gaining weight. However, people who compulsively overeat often are caught in a cycle of bingeing and dieting. They binge for a while, gain weight, feel guilty, go on a diet, and then start bingeing again.

According to the American Psychiatric Association, the six warning signs for binge-eating disorder are:

Eating a lot of food quickly

Bingeing at least twice a week for six months

Bingeing alone

Being unable to stop eating

Feeling depressed and guilty after bingeing; feeling self-hate.

Not purging, fasting, or exercising after bingeing

Eating disorders are a serious health problem. Most people with eating disorders are controlled by, or obsessed with, food. Many think of food constantly—how to get it, how to avoid it, how to get rid of it. They keep their eating behavior a secret from others and deny they have a problem.

Points to Consider

Do you think compulsive overeating could be harmful? Why?

Why do you think people compulsively overeat?

More females than males have eating disorders. Why do you think this is true?

Chapter Overview

Some people may be more at risk than others to compulsively overeat.

Children who learn unhealthy eating habits may be at risk in later years.

Family background may play a role in compulsive overeating.

Young females often try unhealthy diets to achieve model-like thinness. Dieting, however, can backfire and lead to compulsive overeating.

People who are depressed may binge on certain foods that lift their mood for a short time.

Chapter **2**

Who Is at Risk?

Compulsive overeating can develop in anyone. However, some people may be more at risk than others to compulsively overeat.

Learning Unhealthy Habits
People who learn unhealthy eating habits as children may compulsively overeat in later years.

DYLAN, AGE 17, AND CASSIE, AGE 14

Dylan and Cassie compulsively overeat. Growing up, Dylan watched his father take three or four helpings at every meal. His father ate fast and rarely talked during meals. Dylan thought this was the normal way to eat.

As a child, Cassie belonged to the Clean Plate Club. Her parents praised her when she ate everything on her plate. They said she was a good girl. Cassie wanted to please her parents. She learned to eat even though her stomach was full.

Many families use food as a sign of love. For example, a mother may fix a delicious meal to show her family how much she cares about them. She expects the children to eat a lot to show their love and appreciation in return. If the children don't have two or three helpings, they may feel guilty.

"Sometimes I get so mad because I can't lose weight that I just give up and splurge."—Erin, age 15

Parents may use food to comfort a child whose friend moves away or whose pet dies. Food becomes more than a means to satisfy physical hunger. Children learn to connect food with feelings. In some cases, that connection can lead to out-of-control eating.

LeAnn believes that her compulsive overeating began in grade school. Whenever she had a bad day, her mother soothed her feelings with a glass of milk and cookies. LeAnn learned that food could lift her spirits.

LeAnn, Age 17

Family Background

People who grow up in families where food is scarce may compulsively overeat as adults. They may be terrified of being hungry again. They overeat to avoid that empty feeling in their stomach.

A family history of alcohol or other drug abuse also is a risk factor for compulsive overeating. People may inherit a tendency toward addiction. Instead of becoming addicted to alcohol or other drugs, they may become addicted to food.

The term *yo-yo dieting* describes the binge-diet cycle. The weight of people caught in the binge-diet cycle goes up and down. They diet and lose weight, binge and gain weight back, diet again and lose weight, and so on. Yo-yo dieters might gain and lose the same 10 pounds over and over again.

Dieting

Dieting means controlling the amount or type of food eaten, usually for the purpose of losing weight. Dieting to lose weight can trigger binge eating. When people severely limit their food intake, their metabolism changes and they become tired. The speed at which the body burns calories slows down. Feeling hungry and low on energy can make food even more tempting. By the time the person gives in to the hunger, he or she cannot stop eating.

Dieting also is a mental trap. People who go on strict diets generally don't allow themselves to eat food they enjoy. They may find themselves thinking about these foods all the time. When they no longer can resist these foods, they binge.

The Teen Years

Most people who compulsively overeat start losing control during their teen years. Teens, especially girls, are at risk to become compulsive overeaters for two main reasons: They dislike their body shape and weight, and they feel overwhelmed.

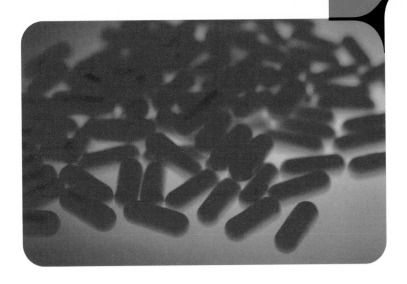

Body Shape and Weight

North Americans are obsessed with fitness and thinness. Movies, TV, and magazines all send the message that beauty means being thin and toned. This ideal is not possible for everyone. People naturally come in a variety of shapes and sizes.

Physical appearance is extremely important to most teens. Girls especially may believe that they must be thin to be popular or attractive. Teens who are unhappy with their body may take unhealthy measures to lose weight. They might go on fad diets or take diet pills. When these measures fail, they may dislike themselves even more. They may turn to food for comfort.

Feeling Overwhelmed

The teen years are full of difficult physical, emotional, and social changes. Teens often lack the experience and skills to deal with these changes. Food is always there for them. It can be trusted. Focusing on food helps some teens forget about their problems, at least for a while.

Eighty percent of all eating disorders start with a diet to lose weight.

Depression

Experts on eating disorders believe that at least half of all people who compulsively overeat are seriously depressed. Depression causes a person to feel extremely sad and hopeless. Research shows that low levels of certain brain chemicals may contribute to depression. Chocolate, sugary foods, and the stimulant caffeine, found in many colas and coffee, contain substances that elevate mood temporarily. Depressed persons may eat large amounts of these foods to feel better.

Daily Habits

A person's habits might lead to compulsive overeating. Some people like to eat while talking on the telephone or watching TV. They may automatically reach for food while doing these activities. It's easy to lose track of how much a person eats during a long conversation or movie.

Today, many families do not have a scheduled time for meals. Many people feel overwhelmed with school, work, and family responsibilities. They often don't have the time or energy to plan meals. Instead, they just grab something to eat on the run. With no set time to eat, many people tend to eat all the time.

Points to Consider

What eating behaviors did you learn as a child? Do you think they were healthy or unhealthy? Why?

Do you know anyone who has tried to lose weight with a fad diet or diet pills? If so, what was the outcome?

Is being thin important to you? Why or why not?

Does your school encourage or discourage healthy eating habits? Explain.

People who compulsively overeat often use food to help themselves feel better when they are upset. They use food to celebrate when they are happy. They also may eat to help themselves forget their problems.

Worry, frustration, boredom, loneliness, and other uncomfortable feelings can trigger binge eating.

People may compulsively overeat to avoid dealing with conflict or to exert control.

Physical, emotional, or sexual abuse can lead to compulsive overeating.

Some people may overeat compulsively because of a physical problem.

Chapter **3**

Looking at the Causes

Experts on eating disorders believe that compulsive overeating has an emotional basis. However, in some cases, biological or physical problems may lead to overeating.

Emotional Causes for Overeating

Food is meant to satisfy physical hunger. It's the fuel that gives you energy to work, study, and play. People also use food for emotional satisfaction. You might be happy because you did well on a math test. You treat yourself to a hot fudge sundae as a reward. You might feel upset because you did poorly on the test. Then the hot fudge sundae becomes a way to make yourself feel better.

It's natural to look to food for pleasure and comfort. People who compulsively overeat, however, use food to an extreme degree to satisfy emotional needs. They may feel that something is missing from their life. They try to fill that emptiness with food.

Uncomfortable Feelings

Worry, frustration, boredom, disappointment, and other uncomfortable feelings can trigger overeating. People who compulsively overeat may use food to find relief from these feelings. In people with low self-esteem, even positive, happy feelings can trigger overeating. They may believe they don't deserve to be happy. To punish themselves, they overeat. Then after a binge, they hate themselves. This only worsens their low self-esteem.

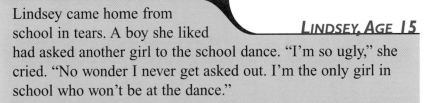

"I wondered why I couldn't stick to a diet and lose weight. 'It's because you're such a loser,' I told myself. For years I punished myself for things I didn't have the courage to stand up to."—Ken, age 18

TEEN TALK

LINDSEY, AGE 15

Lindsey came home from school in tears. A boy she liked had asked another girl to the school dance. "I'm so ugly," she cried. "No wonder I never get asked out. I'm the only girl in school who won't be at the dance."

She went into the kitchen and started looking in the refrigerator for something to eat. Food always made her feel better. In the freezer section, she found a large pepperoni pizza. Lindsey popped it in the oven. Soon the pizza was ready.

Lindsey cut the pizza into large pieces and sat on the floor to eat it. She didn't care that the hot cheese burned her mouth. It just felt so good to eat. In a few minutes, all that remained of the pizza was a scrap of crust.

Response to Conflict

Conflict can be a trigger for overeating. Instead of dealing with a problem, people who compulsively overeat may try to escape a conflict by bingeing. They try to swallow their feelings of anger and frustration as they eat. Food also can be a weapon in a power struggle. Some teens may use overeating as a way to assert themselves with their parents. Overeating may be their indirect way of defying a parent's control.

Colleen and her mother battle over many things. Colleen knows **COLLEEN, AGE 16** that her weight bothers her mother. She tries constantly to get Colleen to slim down. This makes Colleen eat even more.

Covering Up Abuse

People who have been emotionally, physically, or sexually abused may compulsively overeat. They may focus on food to help forget terrible memories or to avoid dealing with ongoing situations. It is not unusual for abuse victims to blame themselves for the abuse. They may use bingeing and gaining weight as a way of punishing themselves.

Saldane gained 100 pounds from two years of compulsive **SALDANE, AGE 18** overeating. She dropped the excess weight through diet and exercise. Soon, however, she started bingeing and gaining weight again. Saldane began to realize that her compulsion was not about food. Instead, it was the result of a terrible event from her past. When she was 16, her former boyfriend and his two friends gang-raped her. She never told anyone. Instead, she found comfort in food.

Compulsive Overeating

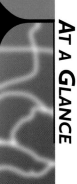

A traumatic event can trigger binge eating. Tennis champion Monica Seles compulsively overate after a rival's fan stabbed her in 1993. She gained 35 pounds within a few months.

Children who have a parent or caregiver who abuses alcohol or other drugs may hide their feelings with food. They may be unable to show in any other way how much the person's behavior hurts them. Often children in such situations mistakenly feel they are responsible for the person's behavior. Then food becomes a way to punish themselves.

Avoiding Sexuality

Some people use food and weight gain to avoid sexual relationships. They may feel uncomfortable about their sexual feelings. They may want to avoid decisions about sexual activity. These people believe that if they are overweight no one will want to have a relationship with them.

Miles gets hunger attacks. He becomes weak, dizzy, and shaky.

MILES, AGE 14

He starts to sweat. Miles must eat right away. He stuffs food in his mouth as fast as he can. He eats and eats until he feels in control of himself.

Biological Causes of Overeating

Miles's eating behavior has a biological basis. He has hypoglycemia, or low blood sugar. He needs a quick supply of sugar to boost his energy level. Hypoglycemia is a condition related to diabetes. This disease involves too much sugar in the blood.

Other biological causes of overeating include:

A chemical or mineral imbalance—A lack of certain chemicals or minerals may cause a person to overeat. For example, some people who binge-eat have too little serotonin. This chemical tells the brain when the stomach is full.

Yeast infection—A fungus causes a yeast infection. It feeds on sugar, causing a person to be hungry for sugary foods.

Food allergies—People with food allergies have a bad reaction to certain foods. Their skin may break out or they may have difficulty breathing. They may get sores in their mouth. Even so, their body may crave the foods it can't handle.

Thyroid disease—The thyroid gland regulates metabolism. An overactive thyroid gland may cause a person to be hungry all the time.

Feelings influence food cravings. If you're nervous, you might keep tossing chips in your mouth. If you're angry, you might want something hard, like pretzels. If you need tender, loving care, you might choose something soft and creamy, like mashed potatoes or pudding. If you're feeling sad and lonely, you might crave sweets.

Points to Consider

Describe a time when you used food to reward yourself or comfort yourself. How did you feel while you were eating? How did you feel afterward?

Give examples of events or happenings that cause uncomfortable emotions in teens. Can overeating be a response to these events? If so, what might be a better way to respond?

Your father grounds you for two weeks because you missed your curfew. You are angry. List three healthy ways you could deal with your anger.

Chapter Overview

People who compulsively overeat almost always gain weight. Being overweight or obese can lead to serious health problems such as heart disease and diabetes. People who are obese also may face prejudice.

Compulsive overeating can damage social relationships. People who compulsively overeat may isolate themselves because of their eating behavior.

Binge eating may ease emotional distress for a short while. In the long run, it almost always leads to more guilt, shame, and unhappiness.

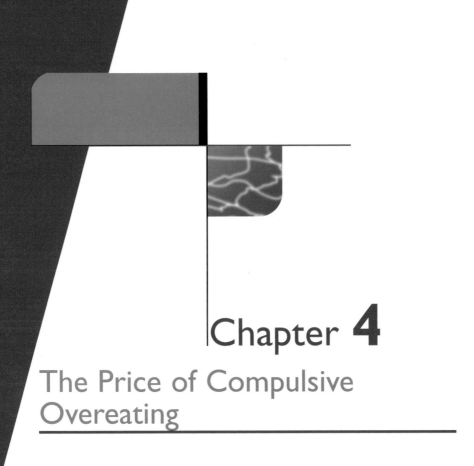

Chapter **4**

The Price of Compulsive Overeating

People who compulsively overeat pay a high price. This disorder may damage their physical health and their social relationships. Their emotional problems may worsen.

Physical Effects of Compulsive Overeating

The most obvious physical consequence of compulsive overeating is weight gain. People who compulsively overeat usually do not exercise to lose weight. For them, dieting tends to trigger binge eating. As a result, most people who compulsively overeat become overweight. Some become obese, or extremely overweight.

According to the National Heart, Lung and Blood Institute, people with a body mass index (BMI) of 25 to 30 are overweight. People with a BMI of 30 and above are obese. BMI is a height-to-weight ratio. To figure out your BMI, multiply your weight in pounds by 703 and multiply your height in inches by your height in inches. Then divide the first answer by the second. Here's an example for a person who is 5 feet 5 inches (65 inches) and weighs 150 pounds:

1. $150 \times 703 = 105{,}450$

2. $65 \times 65 = 4{,}225$

3. $105{,}450 \div 4{,}225 = 24.9$

4. BMI is 24.9

Not all overweight or obese people compulsively overeat. People gain weight for other reasons, too. For example, some people gain weight because of a hormone imbalance. Hormones are chemicals in the body that influence growth and development.

Effect of Obesity on Physical Health

Obesity can lead to serious health problems. When the body carries extra weight, every part is overworked. The heart must work harder to pump blood throughout the body. This increases the risk of high blood pressure, clogged blood vessels, heart attack, and stroke. The skeletal system must strain to support the extra weight. This increases the risk of back problems and injuries to the joints. Obesity can trigger diabetes and make the disease harder to control.

Added weight is not the only way that compulsive overeating can affect health. Repeated bingeing and dieting also upsets the body's metabolism. The foods eaten during a binge often are high in fat and sugar. This means the body does not receive the nutrition it needs.

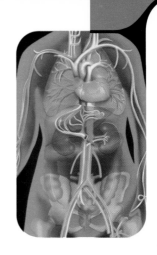

Effect of Obesity on Mental Health

Obesity affects a person's mental health as well. North American culture tends to have a negative view of people who are overweight. They may be rejected when applying for jobs. They can be the target of jokes. Such cruelty can be emotionally painful. It also reinforces, or strengthens, the person's negative self-image.

DEAN, AGE 16

Dean compulsively overeats. He has been overweight most of his life. Dean has heard all the fat jokes and has been called every name. In grade school, other kids picked on him and made fun of him. They told him he was too fat to do this or that.

Now that Dean is in high school, things have gotten a little better. A lot of kids still avoid him, though. Dean would like to start dating girls, but he can't believe any girl would go out with him. "I could go out on a blind date," he says, "but then the girl really would have to be blind."

Dean has learned to defend himself with humor. He makes jokes about his weight before other kids have a chance to say anything. Dean may be laughing on the outside, but inside he's miserable. He sometimes thinks about killing himself.

"People always used to say to me, 'You have such a pretty face. If you'd only lose weight, you'd be so attractive.' They didn't understand that I tried and tried to lose weight. I didn't want to be this way. I needed help."—Deanna, age 17

Social Effects of Compulsive Overeating

Compulsive overeating can prevent a person from having healthy social relationships. People who compulsively overeat may isolate themselves from other people. They may prefer to stay at home alone and binge. They may be afraid they will lose control and binge in public. Dean, for example, didn't want to go to his grandparents' wedding anniversary celebration. He was worried he would pig out in front of his relatives.

The eating behavior of people who compulsively overeat may lead to problems with family members and friends.

Latitia's compulsive overeating has gotten her into lots of trouble. **LATITIA, AGE 14** She frequently daydreams about food in school. Her teachers get mad because she's not paying attention.

Latitia once got caught stealing five dollars from another girl's purse. She wanted the money to buy snack food.

At home, Latitia's behavior upsets her family. When food is missing from the refrigerator, she lies and says her brother's friends ate it. Once she ate half of her brother's birthday cake before his party. Her brother didn't speak to her for a week.

Latitia doesn't want to act like this. She just can't seem to stop herself.

Myth: Fat people are always happy.

Fact: People who are overweight may seem to be happy in order to fit in. Often they are unhappy and depressed.

Emotional Effects of Compulsive Overeating

Compulsive overeating can have a devastating effect on emotions. This disorder creates a vicious emotional cycle. The person overeats because he or she is unhappy. The person gains weight and feels more unhappy and then turns to food for comfort. A person who compulsively overeats may feel better while bingeing. After the binge, however, the problems have not gone away.

Compulsive overeating lowers the person's self-esteem even further. The person may fear accepting new challenges or trying new things because of being overweight. Latitia, for example, would like to try out for the school play. She's afraid, however, that no one wants to see a fat person on stage.

Some people who compulsively overeat may blame all their problems on being overweight. "If only I were thin . . . ," they might say. This type of thinking further limits them and adds to their unhappiness.

Points to Consider

How are students who are overweight treated in your school? Are students who are obese discriminated against?

What can you do to improve attitudes toward people who are overweight?

Why is dieting not the answer to the problems of people who overeat compulsively?

People who compulsively overeat need professional help to overcome their eating disorder. The first step is a physical exam to rule out a biological cause for overeating.

Mental health professionals help people who compulsively overeat to deal with the emotional reasons for bingeing.

Nutrition counselors help people who compulsively overeat adopt a balanced diet and regulate their eating habits.

Support groups can encourage people who compulsively overeat to stop binge eating.

Weight-loss programs generally do not provide the right kind of help for people who compulsively overeat.

Chapter **5**

Choosing Health

People who compulsively overeat need to seek help for the disorder. Treatment differs from person to person. Help is available from doctors, mental health professionals, and nutrition counselors, and from other people with eating disorders.

Medical Doctors

A physical examination is the first step in treating binge-eating disorder. An exam may find a biological cause for the person's overeating. The doctor checks for signs of hypoglycemia, diabetes, thyroid disease, and other conditions. If the cause is biological, the doctor may prescribe medication or changes in the person's diet. Adding vitamin and mineral supplements or eliminating certain foods may correct the problem.

Overcoming an addiction to food may be more difficult than overcoming an addiction to alcohol or other drugs. Alcoholics can remove alcohol from their life and still live. People addicted to food still must eat.

Mental Health Professionals

If a biological reason for compulsive overeating is not found, therapy is the next step. Help is available from a mental health professional such as a psychiatrist or a psychologist. Such professionals are trained to treat emotional and mental illness. Some hospitals have eating disorders clinics. Such clinics may have therapists on staff who have been trained to help treat eating disorders.

The slogan for therapy for compulsive overeating might be "Mood Before Food." The person must first understand the emotional reasons behind compulsive overeating. A therapist helps the person identify the situations or feelings that trigger overeating. The person can learn ways to avoid those triggers. Then the person can find better ways to cope with anger, stress, and other uncomfortable feelings. When abuse or trauma is part of the cause, a therapist can help the person deal with those issues. Trauma is a shocking or upsetting event.

Carmen is in treatment for compulsive overeating. She

learned that part of her problem is her inability to express anger. She stuffs her anger—along with mounds of food—inside herself.

Carmen and her therapist, Dr. Hill, talk about situations that make Carmen angry. He has taught her steps to manage her anger. Carmen has written the steps on a card to remind her what to do.

Recognize that you are angry.

Figure out why you are angry.

Deal directly with the person or situation that makes you angry.

Calmly describe the problem and how it affects you.

Listen to the other side.

Work together toward a solution.

Dr. Hill involves Carmen's family in her therapy. Carmen used the anger-management steps to talk with her parents. They learned that a lot of Carmen's anger comes from being the oldest child and having too many responsibilities at home. They realized that Carmen needs more time for herself.

Therapy for compulsive overeating also includes helping the person do the following:

Overcome negative and distorted thinking, such as "I can't do anything right" or "I'm the only one who won't be at the party"

Build self-esteem

Like himself or herself regardless of appearance

Learn techniques to relax

If the person is depressed, the therapist may prescribe antidepressants. These drugs increase the levels of the brain chemicals that regulate emotions. They can help restore a normal mood to a depressed person.

Nutrition Counselors

Working with a nutrition counselor is another important part of treatment for a person with compulsive overeating. Nutrition counselors show the person how to have a healthy diet and better eating habits.

Compulsive Overeating

It takes at least 15 minutes from the start of chewing to signal the brain that the stomach is full. Eating slowly and chewing thoroughly help prevent overeating. Each bite of food should be chewed 20 times.

Carmen's treatment for

CARMEN SEES A NUTRITION COUNSELOR

compulsive overeating included seeing Jan, a nutrition counselor, once a week. Jan had Carmen start a food diary. Carmen wrote down everything she ate, when she ate it, and how she was feeling at the time. The food diary helped Carmen become more aware of things that triggered her overeating.

Carmen needed to relearn signals of physical hunger. Jan told Carmen to chew her food slowly and thoroughly. This would give her brain time to realize that her stomach was full and that she should stop eating. Jan also encouraged Carmen to adopt these new eating habits:

Eat regular meals each day

Don't skip a meal (going without food creates the urge to binge)

Eat only at the table (no snacking in front of the TV)

Take smaller portions

Don't feel guilty about leaving food on the plate

Carmen wanted Jan to put her on a low-calorie diet to lose weight. Jan said that for now it was more important for Carmen to eat balanced meals. She showed Carmen meal plans that contained plenty of fruits and vegetables. The plans even allowed room for some of Carmen's favorite sweets. Jan said that eating right and exercising—not dieting—was a healthier approach to losing weight.

Overeaters Anonymous was founded in 1960 by three women who had tried many other programs for their eating problems. It is one of the oldest national support groups for eating disorders.

Support Groups

Support groups can play an important role in helping people who compulsively overeat. Getting together with others who share this disorder helps to reduce loneliness and isolation. People who compulsively overeat can learn from others who have the same condition.

Groups can meet daily, weekly, or monthly. Members generally pay little or nothing to attend. They talk about problems they are having and ways they deal with those problems.

One of the best-known support groups is Overeaters Anonymous (OA). This national organization regards food as an addiction much like alcohol or other drugs. OA follows the Twelve Step model created by Alcoholics Anonymous to help people cope with binge-eating disorder. Alcoholics Anonymous is a national organization for people addicted to alcohol or other drugs. About 75 percent of OA's members have binge-eating disorder. Overeaters Anonymous also offers support groups for teens.

Almost one-third of the people who sign up for weight-loss programs have binge-eating disorder.

Weight-Loss Programs

Many people who compulsively overeat turn to weight-loss programs for help. These programs tend to focus on losing weight rather than on the reasons for overeating. Membership fees, weekly meeting fees, and the cost of special food can make these programs expensive.

Points to Consider

What could a family do to help a teen who compulsively overeats?

Why might it be hard for a teen to eat balanced meals and have healthy eating habits?

Do you know anyone who has gone to a weight-loss program? If so, what was the person's experience?

Chapter Overview

It is possible to overcome compulsive overeating with hard work and the support of others.

Denying the problem can be a roadblock to treating compulsive overeating.

People who compulsively overeat have an illness. It is important for them not to feel ashamed to seek help.

Simple overeating can in some cases become a habit that leads to an eating disorder.

Chapter **6**

Maggie's Story

Maggie is a happy, healthy high school junior. This was not always the case. Maggie has compulsively overeaten for much of her life. Her story shows that it is possible to overcome this eating disorder.

Maggie at Risk

Maggie began to develop poor eating habits at age 9. Her parents divorced and her mother began working full time. The family stopped having meals together. Maggie's mother expected Maggie and her older sister to get their own dinner. The girls usually found it easier to munch on snacks.

After a long day at work, Maggie's mother often brought home pastries and fast food to make herself feel better. The food cheered up the girls, too.

Many people think in terms of "good" food and "bad" food. Good food tends to be low in calories and full of vitamins and minerals. Bad food usually is high in calories and full of sugar and fat. People who compulsively overeat may feel guilty and think of themselves as bad if they eat sugary, fatty foods. Nutritionists try to help people avoid judging themselves by the type of food they eat. Nutritionists also do not label food good or bad.

Causes of Maggie's Overeating

Maggie comes from a family that does not easily express emotions. She never learned to talk about things that bothered her. She never told anyone how she felt when her parents divorced. She and her father had been close, and she missed him terribly.

Food gradually became Maggie's only comfort. If she was lonely, she ate. If she was stressed, she ate. Even if she was happy, she ate. When Maggie turned 12, her mother got a new job and the family moved to a different state. The move triggered more feelings of loneliness and insecurity. Food became Maggie's best friend.

Maggie, a Compulsive Overeater

By the time she was 14, Maggie had a serious problem with compulsive overeating. She ate constantly throughout the day. She bought snacks from the school's vending machines and ate them between classes. During class, she popped candy in her mouth when the teacher wasn't looking. When she got home from school, she hid herself in her room to gorge on doughnuts and cupcakes. After dinner, Maggie continued to nibble. She polished off a grocery bag full of junk food every evening.

Being overweight in the teen years can be more dangerous than adult obesity. Excess weight interferes with healthy growth and development. It puts teens at risk for weight-related health problems at an earlier age.

MAGGIE SAYS:

"I fed my mouth even when my stomach was full. It just got to be such a habit. Sometimes I didn't even know I was eating. I felt powerless against food."

Maggie Pays the Price

At 15, Maggie was 5 feet 2 inches tall and weighed 185 pounds. Most of the time she felt miserable. Maggie could not fit into the kinds of clothes the other girls wore. She dressed in dark clothes to make herself look slimmer. Gym class was the worst. Maggie hated to undress and expose her body. She could hear the other girls whisper, "How could she let herself get like that?"

Maggie's weight caused other problems, too. Her back and knees ached from the extra weight she carried. She sometimes had difficulty breathing. Going up the stairs at school left her winded and exhausted. She frequently had cramps and stomachaches. Her face looked pale and puffy.

MAGGIE SAYS:

"I told myself that someday I would stick to a diet. I would lose weight and then everything would be okay."

After bingeing, Maggie felt guilty. She hated herself. Why couldn't she stop? Deep down, she knew something was wrong with her eating behavior. She did not realize it had a name.

Maggie Chooses Health

One day Maggie read an article about eating disorders in a teen magazine. She already knew about anorexia and bulimia. The article talked about compulsive overeating. Maggie felt like she was reading about herself. She suddenly felt a sense of relief. Her problem had a name. It could be treated.

Maggie got up the courage to tell the school nurse about her binges. The nurse arranged for Maggie to work with a nutritionist. The nutritionist had Maggie keep a food diary. Maggie was amazed at the amount of sugary junk food she ate every day.

The nurse recommended that Maggie talk with a therapist about her feelings. Maggie was surprised by the things that came up— things that she never even knew bothered her. She learned that eating had been a way of grieving her parents' divorce. She realized that others' remarks about her size made her want to eat even more. Maggie learned what she could do besides eat to make herself feel better.

Signs that indicate recovery from compulsive overeating:

Having fewer episodes of binge eating or no longer eating constantly

Keeping weight normal or near normal

Eating regular meals with normal amounts of food

Being involved in activities that have nothing to do with food, weight, or appearance

Enjoying relationships with family members and friends

Talking about feelings

MAGGIE SAYS:

"Giving up eating all the time was scary. I felt like I was losing my best friend. But I couldn't use food as a crutch any longer."

Maggie Gets Support

Maggie started going to a support group. She was relieved to hear that other people struggled with food. When Maggie felt upset, she could call another group member. Talking about her feelings helped her avoid overeating.

Maggie's friend Adele provided support, too. Adele made Maggie feel good about getting help. Adele said Maggie was doing the right thing.

Getting the support of Maggie's mother was a different matter. At first, Maggie's mother denied that Maggie had problems with food. She believed that Maggie just enjoyed it more than other people. Family therapy helped convince her that Maggie had an eating disorder.

Maggie Gets Better

After several months, Maggie began to feel better. Over time, she lost 50 pounds without starving herself or taking diet pills. Her weight loss came gradually as she learned to control her eating behavior. She ate meals at regular times. She identified foods that triggered her overeating. Avoiding these foods helped her cut down to three meals a day.

Maggie's exercise program helped, too. She began walking 30 minutes a day, 4 days a week. At first it was hard to make time in her schedule for exercise. Then Maggie realized how good she felt on the days she walked. It didn't take long before she was walking two miles every day.

Today, at 16, Maggie enjoys spending time with her friends. She isn't embarrassed to go clothes shopping anymore. Best of all, Maggie knows how to deal with her feelings. She knows when she is physically full. Maggie realizes that she may struggle with compulsive overeating all her life. She believes, however, that her new lifestyle will help her through.

MAGGIE SAYS:

"I had to change my lifestyle in order to get better. I had to force myself to eat more fruits and vegetables and to exercise. I learned to pay attention to my emotions and figure out what was bothering me. I also learned to speak up for myself."

Points to Consider

How would you react if you found out a friend compulsively overeats?

Is there a difference between a teen who has a big appetite and a teen who compulsively overeats? Why or why not?

Do you think it is more acceptable for a boy to binge-eat than a girl? Why or why not?

Your school is holding a contest to see who can eat the most at one time. Do you think this is a good idea? Why or why not?

Chapter Overview

Everyone needs to be aware of tendencies to overeat. People who have a serious problem with compulsive overeating need to seek professional help.

Teens who compulsively overeat can ask a trusted adult to help them find a treatment program.

Many things can be done to control compulsive overeating. One of the most important is to identify situations, feelings, and foods that trigger binges. Finding a support system, learning to control the urge to binge, and keeping busy are other important ways.

The support of people who care can help a great deal in overcoming binge-eating disorder.

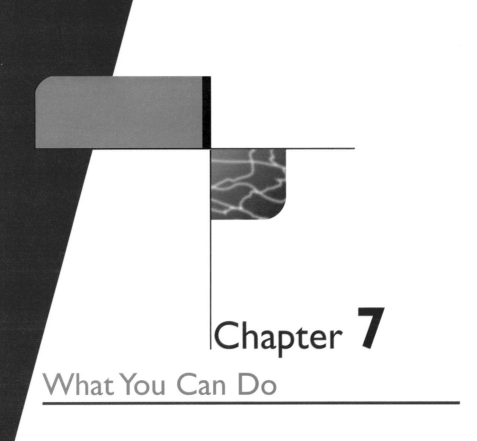

Chapter **7**

What You Can Do

You may be concerned about your own eating habits. You may wonder if you compulsively overeat. If a friend or family member compulsively overeats, you may wonder what to do. This chapter contains suggestions that may help.

Do you think you compulsively overeat? Ask yourself the questions in the following chart.

Do You Compulsively Overeat?		
Answer yes or no to each question.		
Do you find yourself eating constantly, or do you sometimes eat a huge amount of food in a short period? (For example, two or three hamburgers plus two or three orders of fries, followed by a gallon of ice cream.)	YES	NO
Do you ever feel out of control and eat more rapidly than normal during these times?	YES	NO
Do you feel ashamed of your eating behavior and disgusted by your body?	YES	NO
Do you eat normally when you are with others and binge when you are alone?	YES	NO
Do you frequently eat when you are not really hungry at all?	YES	NO
Do you frequently eat beyond the point of fullness?	YES	NO

You may crave a certain food. This food can set off a binge. You start eating it, and pretty soon you're eating other things as well. If you can identify your trigger food and avoid it, you may be able to reduce bingeing.

Do you lie about your eating or hide food and eat it secretly?	YES	NO
Do you go on and off diets, repeatedly losing weight and gaining it back?	YES	NO
Do you find yourself thinking about food all or most of the time?	YES	NO
Do your eating habits interfere with your social life, or does your social life revolve around food?	YES	NO
Do you eat to avoid doing things, to manage stress, or to relieve uncomfortable feelings?	YES	NO
Do you think of eating as one of your only pleasures in life?	YES	NO

If you answered yes to six or more of these questions, you may have a problem with compulsive overeating. If you answered yes to fewer than six questions, you still may have problems with your eating behavior.

If you eat to relieve stress, you might choose creamy, starchy, fatty foods. Examples include bread and butter, peanut butter, mashed potatoes, or macaroni and cheese. The substances in these foods trigger the release of chemicals in your body that help you relax. They even may make you feel sleepy.

Annika is recovering from binge-eating disorder. Sweet food sets off her binges. Annika passes a bakery on her way home from school each day. She realizes that she must find a different route. That way she won't be tempted to stop in and buy jelly-filled doughnuts and chocolate cream puffs.

ANNIKA, AGE 14

Things to Do

If you think you have a problem with compulsive overeating, tell someone. It is important not to feel ashamed. You are not alone. Ask a parent, school counselor, or family doctor to help you find a treatment program. You also can look under *Eating Disorders* in the phone directory. The Useful Addresses and Internet Sites section at the back of this book contains helpful resources as well. Here are more things you can do:

Identify your triggers. Think about situations or feelings that set off your binges. Once you know your triggers, you can take steps to avoid them or deal with them. Writing in a journal can help you figure out what's bothering you.

Find a support system. Be aware that family members may not be able to recognize dangerous eating habits. The organizations listed on page 62 may be able to help you find a support group. Check your phone book under *Eating Disorders* or *Support Groups.* If no groups are available in your area, start one of your own.

Learn to handle the urge to binge. If you feel the urge to eat, wait 15 minutes. This will help you decide if you really are hungry. Ask yourself how you are feeling. Do you want to eat because you feel sad? happy? fearful? If so, switch to a different activity. Telephone a friend, go for a walk, or take a shower. If you do binge, don't be hard on yourself. You will have another chance to be successful.

Break the connection between food and reward. If you use food to reward yourself, treat yourself to something else you want or enjoy. Buy a new CD, go for a bike ride, or work on a hobby.

Keep busy. If you are doing other things, you will be less likely to binge. Do things that you enjoy or that will help you grow as a person. Join a club, take up a sport, or volunteer. Do things with other people. Isolation creates opportunities for bingeing.

Boredom and loneliness caused Blaine's compulsive overeating.

Before he went to therapy, Blaine would come home from school and plop down in front of the TV. Then he would wolf down bags of potato chips and pretzels until his mother came home from work.

His therapist got Blaine involved as a volunteer in an after-school program for kids. Blaine passes out juice and crackers, plays games with the children, and reads to them. The kids love having a big guy around, and Blaine loves being around them. Not only did he stop his after-school bingeing, but also his self-esteem soared.

"One trick I've learned is to brush and floss my teeth often. Having a clean mouth reduces my urge to eat."—Flory, age 17

"I keep a list of things to do when I'm bored. It keeps me from sitting around and eating."—Gus, age 14

"I had to give up my job at a fast-food restaurant. I was putting away too many burgers and fries. Now I work at a shoe store."—Damion, age 17

If You Know Someone Who Compulsively Overeats

It can be difficult to spot compulsive overeating in a friend or family member. Here are some signs to look for. A person who compulsively overeats may:

Gain weight even when he or she eats only small amounts around others

Seem depressed

Cancel appointments or plans with friends

Miss a lot of school or work

Seem upset about his or her weight (for example, he or she may avoid looking in full-length mirrors)

Things to Do

You may believe that a friend or family member has a problem with compulsive overeating. If so, tell the person what you observe. Encourage him or her to get help. You can give support in the following ways.

Don't nag or scold about gaining weight or overeating. This only leads to resentment.

Don't offer advice unless it is asked for. The person probably doesn't want to hear what you would do.

Try not to judge the person. The person needs support, not criticism.

Offer to go along to the person's first support group meeting.

Take the focus off food when you do things with the person. For example, instead of going out for pizza, go for a hike.

Avoid talking about your own weight or dieting.

Focus on personality, not appearance. Compliment the person on traits like kindness or intelligence.

Points to Consider

What steps would you take to get help for compulsive overeating?

How could you help a friend or family member who compulsively overeats?

What can you do to educate others about binge-eating disorder?

Glossary

anorexia (an-uh-REK-see-uh)—an eating disorder in which the person starves himself or herself

binge (BINJ)—to eat a large amount of food in a short period of time

bulimia (buh-LEE-mee-uh)—an eating disorder in which the person binges and purges

calorie (KAL-uh-ree)—a measurement of the amount of energy that a food gives

compulsion (kuhm-PUHL-shuhn)—an uncontrollable urge

depression (di-PRESH-uhn)—a mood disorder in which a person feels extremely sad, hopeless, and helpless

diabetes (dye-uh-BEE-tuhss)—a disease in which a person has too much sugar in the blood

hypoglycemia (hye-poh-glye-SEE-mee-uh)—an abnormal decrease of sugar in the blood

laxative (LAK-suh-tiv)—a drug that loosens waste and helps make bowel movements happen

metabolism (muh-TAB-uh-liz-uhm)—the process by which the body changes food into energy

nutrition (noo-TRISH-uhn)—food and substances people need to stay strong and healthy

obesity (oh-BEE-suh-tee)—the condition of being extremely overweight

obsession (uhb-SESH-uhn)—an idea, a thought, or an emotion that is always on a person's mind

purge (PURJ)—to rid the body of excess food, usually by vomiting or using laxatives

therapy (THER-uh-pee)—treatment designed to improve a person's health or well-being

For More Information

Bode, Janet. *Food Fight: A Guide to Eating Disorders for Pre-Teens and Their Parents.* New York: Simon & Schuster, 1997.

Folkers, Gladys. *Taking Charge of My Mind and Body.* Minneapolis: Free Spirit, 1997.

Graves, Bonnie. *Anorexia.* Mankato, MN: Capstone Press, 2000.

Graves, Bonnie. *Bulimia.* Mankato, MN: Capstone Press, 2000.

Ward, Christie L. *Compulsive Eating: The Struggle to Feed the Hunger Inside.* New York: Rosen, 1998.

Useful Addresses and Internet Sites

American Dietetic Association
216 West Jackson Boulevard
Chicago, IL 60606
Nutrition Hot Line
1-800-366-1655
www.eatright.org

Eating Disorders Awareness and Prevention
(EDAP)
603 Stewart Street
Suite 803
Seattle, WA 98101
1-800-931-2237
www.edap.org

The National Eating Disorders Information
Centre
200 Elizabeth Street, CW1-211
Toronto, ON M5G 2C4
CANADA
www.nedic.on.ca

New Realities Eating Disorders Recovery
Centre
62 Charles Street East
Toronto, ON M4Y 1T1
CANADA
www.newrealitiescan.com

Overeaters Anonymous Headquarters
6075 Zenith Court Northeast
Rio Rancho, NM 87124
www.overeatersanonymous.org

Eating Disorders Shared Awareness
Mirror-Mirror
www.mirror-mirror.org/eatdis.htm
Facts about eating disorders, recovery, and
self-tests for eating disorders

The Fat-Fairy Godmother's Website
www.fatfairygodmother.com/index.htm
Advice on how to change thinking about diets
and dieting, affirmations, and a self-quiz

Health Information Page at the University of
Alberta
www.ualberta.ca/dept/health/public_html
/healthinfo/bodyim.html
Fights the myths about weight and body image

Nutrition Management Services
www.nms.on.ca/eating_disorders.htm
Information about eating disorders and other
eating issues

Peace It Together
www.mcet.edu/peace/spr3/teen2.html
Advice for and from teens about compulsive
overeating and how to deal with it

Something Fishy
www.something-fishy.org/edlisam.htm
Information about eating disorders, prevention,
and recovery

Index